Patrick Byrne, Theobald Wolfe Tone

Catholics

An Argument on Behalf of the Catholics of Ireland

Patrick Byrne, Theobald Wolfe Tone

Catholics
An Argument on Behalf of the Catholics of Ireland

ISBN/EAN: 9783744704304

Printed in Europe, USA, Canada, Australia, Japan

Cover: Foto ©Lupo / pixelio.de

More available books at **www.hansebooks.com**

CATHOLICS.

AN

ARGUMENT

ON BEHALF OF THE

CATHOLICS OF IRELAND.

IN WHICH

THE PRESENT POLITICAL STATE OF THAT
COUNTRY, AND THE NECESSITY OF A PARLI-
AMENTARY REFORM ARE CONSIDERED.

ADDRESSED TO

THE PEOPLE, AND MORE PARTICULARLY TO THE
PROTESTANTS OF IRELAND.

DUBLIN:

PRINTED BY P. BYRNE, No. 108, GRAFTON-STREET.

M,DCC,XCI.

TO THE READER.

I N the following Pamphlet I have omitted all general arguments in favour of a Parliamentary Reform, which equally apply to England and Ireland ; and have confined myfelf almoft entirely to fuch as exclufively apply to our own country. The general queftion has been fo often and fo ably handled, that the public mind is fufficiently informed; and it is by no means my wifh to fwell my book, and fatigue my Readers, by compiling arguments, which, however powerful, have been repeated, until we may pronounce, that if they have not convinced, conviction is hopelefs. I have argued, therefore, little on the abftract right of the people to reform their

Legiflature ;

Legiflature ; for, after PAINE, who will, or who need, be heard on the fubject ?

IT may be neceffary to premife, that when I ufe the term *Government*, I do not mean by it the Legiflature, as it exifts in theory, but a certain junto of men, of both countries, fome of them Members of our Legiflature, and others not, who poffefs the fupreme power in this country.

TO THE PEOPLE.

BEFORE I proceed to the object of this book, I think it neceffary to acquaint the Reader, that I am a Proteftant of the Church of Ireland, as by law eftablifhed, and have again and again taken all the cuftomary oaths by which we fecure and appropriate to ourfelves all degrees and profeffions, fave one, to the utter exclufion of our Catholic Brethren. I am, therefore, no further interefted in the event, than as a mere lover of juftice, and a fteady detefter of tyranny, whether exercifed by one man or one million.

THE prefent ftate of Ireland is fuch, as is not to be paralleled in hiftory or fable: Inferior to no country in Europe in the

gifts

gifts of nature, bleſt with a temperate ſky and a fruitful ſoil, interſected by many great rivers, indented round her whole coaſt with the nobleſt harbours, abounding with all the neceſſary materials for unlimited commerce, teeming with inexhauſtible mines of the moſt uſeful metals, filled by 4,000,000 of an ingenious and a gallant people, with bold hearts, and ardent ſpirits; poſted right in the track between Europe and America, within 50 miles of England, 300 of France; yet with all theſe great advantages, unheard of and unknown, without pride, or power, or name, without ambaſſadors, army, or navy; not of half the conſequence in the empire of which ſhe has the honour to make a part, with the ſingle county of York, or the loyal and well regulated town of Birmingham!

THESE are, or ſhould be, to every true Iriſhman, mortifying conſiderations: It remains to examine what can be the cauſe of our ſo ſhameful depreſſion, to diſcover and to apply with temper and with firmneſs the remedy; and thus to reſtore, or if not reſtore, to create a rank for our country among the nations of the earth.

THE

THE proximate caufe of our difgrace is our evil government, the remote one is our own inteftine divifion, which, if once removed, the former will be inftantaneoufly reformed.

IT is neceffary for the phyfician to know the diforder, and it is folly to conceal it from the patient himfelf. If he has the fpirit of a man, he will hear the worft with intrepidity, and bear it with fortitude: Death is very terrible, but there are things more terrible than death.

THE misfortune of Ireland is, that we have *no National Government*, in which we differ from England, and from all Europe. In England the King is refident, and his prefence begets infinite advantages ; the Government is Englifh, with Englifh views and interefts only; the people are very powerful, though they have not their due power : whoever is, or would be Minifter, can fecure or arrife at office only by ftudying and following their will, their paffions, and their very prejudices : Hence the interefts of King, Minifters, and People, move forward in one and the fame direction, advanced or retarded by the fame means, and cannot even in idea be feparated.

BUT

BUT is it fo in Ireland?

WHAT is our Government? It is a phe-
nomenon in politics, contravening all re-
ceived and eftablifhed opinions : It is a
Government derived from another country, whofe intereft, fo far from being the
fame with that of the people, directly
croffes it at right angles : Does any man
think that our rulers here recommend
themfelves to their creators in England,
by promoting the interefts of Ireland, when
it can in the moft remote degree interfere
with the commerce of Great Britain ? *
But how is this foreign Government main-
tained? Look to your court calendar, to your
penfion lift, to your concordatum, and you
will find the anfwer written in *letters of*

* If this be doubted, let the proceedings of laft fef-
fion with regard to the Arigna Iron Works and the
Double Loom be remembered, to each of which the
fmalleft parliamentary aid was refufed. Why? Becaufe
they might interfere with Englifh interefts ; though the
former would have kept 250,000*l.* annually at home, the
greater part of which goes to England ; and the latter
would at once have doubled the weaving power of the
kingdom in the linen, filk, and callico branches. But
above all, let the memorable debate on the Eaft India
Trade be recalled, when Adminiftration boldly threw off
the mafk, and told Ireland fhe fhould have no fuch trade,
becaufe it might interfere with the intereft of England.
☞ *They have fuch a trade in America, and they deferve to
have it.*

gold :

gold: This unnatural influence muſt be
ſupported by profligate means, and hence
corruption is the only medium of Government in Ireland. The people is utterly
difregarded and defied: Divided and dif-
tracted as they are, and diſtruſtful of each
other, they fall an eaſy prey to Engliſh
rulers, or their Iriſh ſubalterns : The fear
of danger is removed from Adminiſtration
by our internal weakneſs, and the ſenſe of
ſhame ſpeedily follows it : Hence it is,
that we ſee Peculation protected, Venality
avowed, the Peerage proſtituted, the Commons corrupted. We ſee all this at the
very hour, when every where but in Ireland reform is going forward, and level-
ling ancient abuſes in the duſt. Why are
theſe things ſo ? Becauſe Ireland is ſtruck
with a political paralyſis, that has wither-
ed her ſtrength, and cruſhed her ſpirit :
She is not half alive, one ſide is ſcarce animated, the other is dead ; ſhe has by her
own law, as it were, amputated her right
hand ; ſhe has outrun the Goſpel precept,
and caſt her right eye into the fire, even
before it has offended her : Religious intolerance and political bigotry, like the tyrant Mezentius, bind the living Proteſtant
to the dead and half corrupted Catholic,

B   and

and beneath the putrid mafs, even the embryo of effort is ftifled : When the nation is thus circumftanced, it is not to be wondered at, if even an adminiftration of boobies and blockheads prefume to infult, and pillage, and contemn, and defy her.

UNDER fuch an Adminiftration, if God Almighty could in his wrath fuffer fuch an one long to exift, the virtue and the talents of the land would be blafted in the bud. No Irifhman of rank could become a member or fupporter of Government, without at once renouncing all pretenfions to common decency, honefty, or honour: All great endowments of the mind, all lofty fentiments of the foul would be neceffarily and eternally excluded ; and the Government, when once in fuch hands, muft remain fo; political vice, like the principle of fermentation, would propagate itfelf, and contaminate every fucceeding particle, until the fury of an enraged people, or the juft anger of offended Heaven fhould at length, by one blow, deftroy or annihilate the whole polluted mafs !

BUT to quit hypothetic fpeculation, and defcend to facts :

I HAVE faid, that we have *no National Government*. Before the year 1782, it was

not

not pretended that we had, and it is at leaft a curious, if not an ufeful fpeculation, to examine how we ftand in that regard now. And I have little dread of being confuted, when I affert, that all we got by what we are pleafed to dignify with the name of *Revolution,* was fimply, *the means of doing good according to law, without recurring to the great rule of nature, which is above all pofitive ftatutes :* Whether we have done good or not, and if not, why we have omitted to do good is a ferious queftion : The pride of the nation, the vanity of individuals concerned, the moderation of fome honeft men, the corruption of knaves I know may be alarmed, when I affert, that the Revolution of 1782, was the moft bung· ling, imperfect bufinefs, that ever threw ridicule on a lofty epithet, by affuming it unworthily : It is not pleafant to any Irifhman to make fuch a confeffion, but it cannot be helped if truth will have it fo : It is much better that we fhould know and feel our real ftate, than delude ourfelves or be gulled by our enemies with praifes, which we do not deferve, or imaginary bleffings which we do not enjoy.

I LEAVE to the admirers of that era to vent flowing declamations on its theore-

tical

tical advantages, and its viſionary glories;
it is a fine ſubject, and peculiarly flatter-
ing to my countrymen; many of whom
were actors, and almoſt all ſpectators of
it. Be mine the unpleaſing taſk to ſtrip it
of its plumage and its tinſel, and ſhew
the naked figure: The operation will be
ſevere; but if properly attended to, may
give us a ſtrong and ſtriking leſſon of
caution and of wiſdom.

THE Revolution of 1782, was a Revolution which enabled Iriſhmen to ſell at a
much higher price their honour, their integrity, and the intereſts of their country;
it was a Revolution, which, while at one
ſtroke it doubled the value of every bo-
rough-monger in the kingdom, left three-
fourths of our countrymen ſlaves as it found
them, and the Government of Ireland in
the baſe and wicked, and contemptible
hands, who had ſpent their lives in de-
grading and plundering her; nay, ſome
of whom had given their laſt vote decidedly,
though hopeleſsly, againſt this our famous
Revolution: Who of the veteran enemies
of the country loſt his place or his penſion?
who was called forth to ſtation or office
from the ranks of oppoſition? not one!
The power remained in the hands of our
enemies, again to be exerted for our ruin,

with

with this difference, that formerly we had
our diſtreſſes, our injuries, and our inſults
gratis, at the hands of England; but now
we pay very dearly to receive the ſame
with aggravation, through the hands of
Iriſhmen ;—yet this we boaſt of, and call a
Revolution.

SEE how much the ſtrength of *the people*
has been augmented by the arrangement
of 1782! For two ſucceſſive ſeſſions, we
have ſeen meaſures of the moſt undeniable
benefit, and the moſt unqualified neceſſity
to the country, enforced by all the efforts
of the moſt conſummate ability, and re-
pelled without even the ſhadow of argument by Adminiſtration; an Adminiſtration, conſiſting numerically of the individuals who had oppoſed the extenſion of
your commerce in 1779, and the amelio-
ration of your conſtitution in 1782. You
find, or you are utterly ſenſeleſs, in the
loſs of the Place Bill, the Reſponſibility
Bill, the Penſion Bill; in a word, all the
meaſures of laſt ſeſſion, that you have no
weight whatſoever, that Adminiſtration
deſpiſe and laugh at you, and that while
you remain in your preſent ſtate of apathy
and ignorance, they will continue to inſult
and to contemn you.

WHY

WHY do I ſpeak thus of your famous exertions in 1782 ? Not to depreciate them below their value, for I honour, and I love the ſpirit that then animated you. I am ſure a great majority of thoſe who then conducted you, were actuated by a ſincere regard to your intereſt and your freedom; I am ſure that ſome of your leaders were men of high integrity, and ſome of conſummate wiſdom; I do believe that as much, or very nearly as much as could then be done, was done; and though I regret, yet I do not accuſe the caution that induced thoſe who acted for you, to ſtop ſhort in their honourable career : The minds of men were not at that time, perhaps, ripe for exertions, which a thouſand circumſtances that have ſince happened, cry aloud for : We are now, I hope, wiſer, bolder, and more liberal, and we have the great miſtreſs, dear-bought Experience, to warn us from paſt errors, and guide us on to future good.

I HOPE it appears from what I have ſaid, that the Revolution of 1782, is ſuch, as no Iriſhman of an independent ſpirit, and who feels for the honour and intereſt of his country, can acquieſce in *as final.* Much remains to be done, and it is fortunate

nate that the end propofed is fo moderate and juft, the means fo fair, fimple, and conftitutional, as to leave no ground for accufation with the moft profligate of our enemies, or apprehenfion with the moft timid of our friends.

MY argument is fimply this : That Ireland, as deriving her government from another country, requires a ftrength in the people which may enable them, if necef-fary, to counteract the influence of that government, fhould it ever be, as it indifputably has been, exerted, to thwart her profperity : That this ftrength may be moft conftitutionally acquired, and fafely and peaceably exerted through the medium of a Parliamentary Reform : And finally, that no reform is honourable, practicable, efficacious, or juft, which does not include as a fundamental principle, the extenfion of elective franchife to the Roman Catholics, under modifications hereafter to be mentioned.

I BEG I may not be mifunderftood or mifreprefented in my firft pofition. When I talk of Englifh influence being predominant in this country, I do not mean to de-rogate from the due exertion of his Majefty's prerogative : I owe him allegiance,

and

and if occasion should require it, I would
be ready chearfully to spill my blood in his
service; but the influence I mean, is not
as between the King and his subjects, in
matter of prerogative, but as between the
government and people of England, and
the government and people of Ireland, in
matter of trade and commerce : I trust in
God, we owe the English nation no allegiance ; nor is it yet treason to assert, as I
do, that she has acquired, and maintains an
unjustifiable and dangerous weight and influence over the councils of Ireland, whose
interest, wherever it clashes, or appears
to clash with hers, must immediately give
way : Surely this is no question of loyalty.
The King of England is King also of Ireland ; he is in theory, and I trust in
practice, equally interested in the welfare
of both countries ; he cannot be offended
that each of his kingdoms should by all
honourable and just means encrease their
own ability, to render him the service due
to him ; he cannot rejoice, when he hears
that his faithful Commons of Ireland by their
own law exclude themselves from a commerce with half the known world, in com-
plaisance to a monopolizing English company, though he may, as the common father of
both

both his realms, rejoice, when they vote 200,000l. to fecure the very commerce in which they can never bear a part. It is therefore, I repeat it, no queftion of loyalty: If the King can be interefted in the queftion, it muft be ˌon the fide of juftice, and of Ireland, becaufe his happinefs and his pride muft be moft gratified by the rifing profperity of his people, to which title we have as much claim as the people of England ; we love him as well, we are as faithful fubjects; and if we render him not as effential fervices, let our means be confidered, and the blighting influence which perpetually vifits the harveft of our hopes, and I believe it will be found, that our zeal in his fervice is only circumfcribed by our inability.

IT is, therefore, extremely poffible for the moft truly loyal fubject in this kingdom deeply to regret, and confcientioufly to oppofe the domineering of Englifh influence, without trenching in the fmalleft degree on the rational loyalty, fo long and fo juftly the boaft of Ireland: His loyalty is to the King of Ireland, not to the Honourable United Company of Merchants trading, where he muft never trade, to the Eaft Indies : Nor is it to the Clothiers in York-

fhire,

fhire, nor the Weavers of Manchefter, nor yet to the conftitutional reforming Black-fmiths of Birmingham, that he owes allegiance : His firft duty is to his country, his fecond to his King, and both are now, and by God's bleffing will, I hope, remain united and infeparable.

IN England we find a reform in Parliament is always popular, though it is but as a barrier againft poffible, not actual grievance : The people fuffer in theory by the unequal diftribution of the elective franchife; but practically, it is perhaps vifionary to expect a Government that fhall more carefully or fteadily follow their real interefts. No man can there be a Minifter on any other terms. But reform in Ireland is no fpeculative remedy for poffible evils : The Minifter and the Government here hold their offices by a tenure very different from that of purfuing the public good. The people here are defpifed or defied ; their will does not weigh a feather in the balance, when Englifh influence, or the intereft of their rulers, is thrown into the oppofite fcale. We have all the reafons, all the juftice that Englifh reformifts can advance, and we have a thoufand others, that in England never could exift : We

have

have in common with England the royal influence, and the ambition of Minifters to encounter ; but we have alfo the jealous interference of that country to meet in every branch of trade, every department of commerce ; and what barriers have we to oppofe in our prefent ftate of reprefentation ? None : Of *four* millions of people, three are actually and confeffedly unreprefented ; of the remaining fourth, the electors do not exceed 60,000, and the members whom they return, fuppofing them all, what I wifh with truth we could, men of integrity, muft remain for ever a mino‧rity, for their number amounts but to 82.

I FEAR I am wafting time in proving an axiom : Need more be faid, than that a nation governed by herfelf will purfue her interefts more fteadily, than if fhe were governed by another, whofe intereft might clafh with hers ? Is not this more applicable, if the governing nation has a means of perpetrating the mifchief without much odium, by making the governed facrifice her interefts with her own hand ? And can we deny that this is the cafe with Ireland ? I may be told that we are not governed by England, and fome proud and hot-brained Irifhman will again throw

acrofs

acrofs me the *Revolution of* 1782, wherein
we " *glorioufly afferted our claim to legif-*
" *late externally, as well as internally, for*
" *ourfelves:* And I will admit, that we did
affert our claim, but I deny that we have
availed ourfelves of the exertion of the
right: We are free in theory, we are
flaves in fact : When high prerogative
was tumbled to the ground, gentle influence fucceeded, and with infinitely lefs
noife and buftle, retains us in our bonds :
Before 1782, England bound us by her
edict ; it was an odious and not a very fafe
exertion of power ; *but it coft us nothing :*
Since 1782, we are bound by Englifh influence, acting through our own Parliament ; we cannot in juftice accufe her,
for fhe is only to be traced by the mifchief fhe filently and fecretly diftributes ;
but our fuffering is aggravated by this gall-
ing circumftance, that we purchafe re-
ftriction of trade, and invafion of conftitution, at a very dear rate : Englifhmen,
under the old conftitution, would ruin Ireland without fee or reward ; their motive
was to ferve their own country ; but Irifhmen, under the new conftitution, will not
prefer the intereft of England to that of
Ireland,

Ireland, without weighty confiderations ; they expect, and indeed not without fome colour of juftice, to be paid extravagantly for the daily parricide they commit againft the land which gave them birth ; and to complete this difhonourable traffic, the purchafe of their votes comes, not from the pocket of England, who is to benefit, but of Ireland, who is ruined by the fale.

THE Volunteers and people of Ireland were very foon after their imaginary Revolution, made, by grievous experience, fenfible of the truth of what I have now afferted ; they faw the extent of this alarming difeafe, and they as foon difcovered the caufe and the remedy. They faw they had, literally, no weight in the Government, and they clamoured for what, even on the limited plan then propofed, would at leaft have mitigated the diforder—a *Parliamentary Reform.* But they built on too narrow a foundation, and the fuperftructure naturally overfet, when it was fcarcely raifed above the ground : They fet out with facrificing the eternal dictates of juftice, to temporizing and peddling expediency ; they failed, because they did not deferve to fucceed.— Grafping at too much, they loft all ; and

the

the fatal morning, when the Convention broke up at the Rotunda, in one moment demolifhed the glory, which five years of virtuous fuccefs had flattered them would be immortal.

I HAD the misfortune to fee them on the day of their difgrace, when the great bubble burft, and carried rout and confufion, and difmay, among their ranks; when *three hundred* of the firft gentlemen of Ireland, girt with fwords, the reprefentatives of the armed force of the kingdom, who by giving independence, had given to their Parliament the means of being virtuous, fled like deer to their counties, to return no more, after making a foolifh profeffion of their pacific intentions ; foolifh, becaufe it was evident that their anxiety was how they fhould reach their homes, without attachments and incarceration. I faw with forrow their great leader obliged to defcend to the farce of intreating them to form no rafh refolution againft that Government, which had in effect fcourged them home in a ftate of ridiculous diftrefs and obloquy; and I wondered then, like a young man, why fuch men, fo circumftanced, with the eyes of Europe upon them,

them, fhould fubmit quietly to treatment, which a few years experience has fhewn was inevitable; they were difgraced, becaufe they were illiberal, and degraded, becaufe they were unjuft; through them the honor of their country was wounded, her name funk, her glories forgotten, and from the laft day of the Convention, there has been *no people in Ireland.*

FROM their failure we are taught this falutary truth, that no reform can ever be obtained, which fhall not comprehenfively embrace Irifhmen of all denominations: The exclufion of the Catholics loft the queftion under circumftances, that muft have otherwife carried it againft all oppofition; the people were then ftrong and confident, they had arms in their hands, and were in habits of fucceeding; the fame circumftances cannot eafily be fuppofed again to combine in their favour; but if they did, they muft again fail.

THE Almighty fource of wifdom, and of goodnefs, has infeparably connected liberty and juftice : We muft adopt or reject them together ; to be completely free, we muft deferve to be fo : It could not be confiftent with his impartial love to all his creatures, that a monopolizing Ariftocracy fhould

fhould fucceed in wrefting their unalien-
able rights from their oppreffors, at the
moment they were acting the oppreffors
themfelves to millions of their fellow-fub-
jects.

The queftion now refolves itfelf into this.
Shall we be content to remain in our prefent oppreffed and inglorious ftate, unknown and unheard of in Europe, the prey
of England, the laughing-ftock of the
knaves, who plunder us? Or fhall we tem-
perately and conftitutionally exert our
power to procure a complete and radical
emancipation to our country, by a reform
in the reprefentation of the people? If we
chufe the former, then are Irifhmen form-
ed of materials, whofe nature I cannot,
and do not wifh to underftand : It is hopelefs attempting to work on fuch fpirits;
but if they be of human feeling, if they
partake of the common nature of man, if
injuftice and oppreffion have not extinguifhed every fentiment which raifes us above
the beafts that perifh, and makes us feel
that our exiftence is an emanation from
the Divinity, then will I believe that my
countrymen are not yet loft and buried in
hopelefs defperation; that to roufe them

to

to exertion, it is but neceffary to point out their duty, to excite them to juftice, to fhew them what is juft.

LET us, for God's fake, fhake off the old woman, the tales of our nurfes, the terrors of our grandams from our hearts; let us put away childifh fears, look our fitu-ation in the face like men; let us fpeak to this ghaftly fpectre of our diftempered imagination, the genius of Irifh Catholi-city! We fhall find it vanifh away like other phantoms of the brain, diftempered by fear:

" HENCE, horrible fhadow; unreal
" mock'ry, hence!"

THE apprehenfions of moft well meaning and candid Proteftants, for of the bigots in that religion, as in every other, I make no account, when they ferioufly refolve them into their principles, I believe gene-rally terminate in two. Firft, the danger to the church eftablifhment; and fecondly, which they much more ferioufly appre-hend, the refumption of Catholic forfeit-ures; and of courfe fetting the property of the kingdom afloat.

To both thefe apprehenfions I anfwer, that the liberation of the Catholics will be a work of compact, and like all other com-

D   pacts,

pacts, fubject to ftipulations. It will be for the wifdom and moderation of both parties to concede fomewhat ; allowance muft be made on the one hand for the difficult facrifice of parting with power, obtained in injuftice, and long held by force; on the other hand there may be fomething to be pardoned in men condemned to ignorance by the law of the land, and whofe minds have for a century been irri‑ tated by injuries, and inflamed by open infults, or ftill more offenfive connivance and toleration.

But here a good old Proteftant lady will tell me, that all compacts between us are in vain, for no faith, nor even oaths, are to be kept with heretics ; and I know fhe will have many to coincide in opinion with her. But if fhe be right, I marvel that the oath of an Irifh Papift fhould ever be taken in a court of juftice ; yet I have my‑ felf feen it done, before a Proteftant Judge and Jury, who decided, as if the witnefs were actually credible, and without en‑ quiry into the articles of his faith. What becomes of the wifdom of the Legiflature, that has been able to devife no better means for the exclufion of Catholics, from

the

the profeffions and parliament, than oaths
which, as not being in their confcience
binding, might be taken and broken without offence? Yet we find, and to our infinite
lofs, that thefe oaths are to Catholics fo for-
midable, fo ferious, and fo obligatory, that
they are content to renounce profit, honour, freedom, and even their country,
rather than take them. Surely, if faith is
not to be kept with hcretics, there is not
a Catholic in the kingdom but might be in
Parliament to-morrow, had he no obfta·
cle but the oaths to encounter. If therefore, three millions of people have for
near a century chofen to remain in *abfolute
flavery,* rather than take certain oaths
which they thought militated with their
confciences ; I truft, and believe there is
an end of the argument, that oaths to heretics are not binding; an affertion the
moft artful and wicked that ever was de-
vifed, becaufe it perpetually recurs on the
unfortunate Catholic, who in vain may
proteft and fwear, that it is falfe, and that
he abjures and utterly denies it ; ftill may
the good Proteftant with-hold his belief,
for " *faith is not to be kept with heretics.*"
I wonder it never occurred to the inventors
and fupporters of this abominable flander,

D 2

which

which at once cuts up by the roots all confidence between man and man, that they might at laſt convert and convince the Catholics of its truth, or at leaſt drive them to the fallacious principle of not being ſuſpected for nothing ; a principle, which, if they were once to adopt, where is the Proteſtant intereſt of Ireland?

BUT to drop this argument, which indeed ſcarcely deſerves conſideration : Let us ſee the actual ſtate of property, and of the Catholics in Ireland at this day.

THE old families, the original proprietors of the ſoil, who were diſpoſſeſſed and ruined by forfeitures, have long ſince fallen into decay : The repreſentatives of a very great majority of them are, and have been in penury and ignorance, at the ſpade and the plough, without deeds or muniments of their eſtates for a century back : I do not ſay that this is univerſally the caſe ; but I am ſure it is with an infinite majority : In the mean time, while the eſtates have been in Proteſtant hands, the Catholics who had made money by trade, the only road to wealth that was not blocked up againſt them by law, had no way to lay it out but in mortgages, many of them on thoſe very lands. Since the
relaxation

relaxation of the penal laws, many Catholics hold profitable leases under those tenures; many have purchased under the faith of those various acts of attainder and settlement, the repeal of which is assumed as the instant and necessary consequence of admitting Catholics to the rights of citizens. Is it to be thought that the wealthy and respectable part of the Catholics would promote or permit the unspeakable confusion in property, that would result from such a measure as is imputed to them; and this from no motive, but an abstract love of mere justice operating against their own obvious interest, and against a known law of the land, which says, that sixty years possession, however acquired, is a good foundation of property against all mankind : I hope it will not be asserted, that it would be the wish of the Catholics utterly to subvert all law; and in the very worst event, if they were mad and wicked enough to frame the wish, they could not have the power. The wealthy and moderate party of their own persuasion, with the whole Protestant interest, would form a barrier against invasion of property, strong and solid enough to satisfy and remove the doubts of the wise, the apprehensions of the cautious,

the

the fears of the cowardly, every thing but the intolerance of the Proteſtant bigot, and the affected terror and real corruption of the Engliſh Partiſan, who would ſee in the cordial union, and conſolidated ſtrength of Ireland, the downfall of his hopes, and the ruin of the profligate market of his vote and his intereſt.

BUT it will be ſaid, that the Catholics are ignorant, and therefore incapable of liberty ; and I have heard men of more imagination than judgment, make a flouriſhing declamation on the danger of blinding them, by ſuddenly pouring a flood of light on their eyes, which for a century have been buried in darkneſs : To the poetry of this I make no objection, but what is the common ſenſe or juſtice of the argument ? We plunge them by law, and continue them by ſtatute, in groſs ignorance, and then we make the incapacity we have created, an argument for their excluſion, from the common rights of man ! We plead our crime in juſtification of itſelf : If ignorance be their condemnation, what has made them ignorant ? Not the hand of Nature : For I preſume they are born with capacities, pretty much like
other

other men : It is the iniquitous and cruel
injuftice of Proteftant bigotry, that has
made them ignorant ; they are excluded
by law from the poffibility of education ;
for I will not call the liberal connivance of
the heads of our Univerfity, who fuffer,
perhaps by a ftrain on their ftrict duty, a
few to fmuggle a little of that learning,
which is contraband to an Irifh Papift, I will
not, I fay, allow that to be fuch an education as every Irifhman has a right to demand ; they cannot obtain degrees ; thofe
are paled in from them by oaths, *thofe
oaths of which they are fo regardlefs*, and
therefore we find they do not enter our
Univerfity : If Irifh Catholics be bigots to
their religion; if that bigotry which makes
them dangerous, refults from ignorance,
furely it is the duty of a confcientious Legiflature, to labour by every means to remove the caufe, and the effect will of itfelf ceafe ; but it is not the policy of their
oppreffors to part with an argument, of
which they make fo excellent ufe ; and
therefore it is, that the Irifh Catholic clergy are driven into foreign countries to pick
up as they may, a wretched, rambling kind
of inftitution, that deferves not the name

of

of education. Can it be wondered, if the flock be not well taught by fuch paftors; what can they learn, when thus exiled from their native country, but foreign habits and foreign prejudices? What love can they feel for that conftitution, what refpect can they preach for thofe laws which have driven them forth as vagabonds over Europe? Will any Catholic gentle· man fubmit to this? No? And what follows? That which daily experience fhews to be one of the heavy misfortunes of Ireland, the confciences, the morals, and the religion of the bulk of the nation, are in the hands of men of low birth, low feelings, low habits, and no education. But furely, the wretched Prieft, and his ftill more miferable flock, are not to be punifhed for the crime of ignorance, with which, as a peftilence, they have been vifited by the unmitigable rage of Proteftant perfecution. Give them education, open their eyes, fhew them what is law, in fome other form than that of a penal ftatute; give them franchife, as you have already in a certain degree given them property; let them be citizens, let them be *men*.

BUT they are not prepared for liberty? What do we mean by *prepared for liberty?*

Was

Was the Polifh nation prepared for liberty,
when it was planted in one day? Were the
French prepared for liberty ? Yes, I fhall
be told, the Gentry were ; and I anfwer,
fo are the Catholic Gentlemen of Ireland ;
the peafantry of all countries are alike,
with an exception in favour of England,
and that exception fpringing from liberty :
They will follow their leaders ; but I fay,
the Catholic Gentlemen of Ireland have
had advantages of information far beyond
either the Poles or the French, becaufe they
have lived in its neighbourhood, and feen
that in practice which they knew but in
fpeculation : Had Mirabeau waited to *prepare* his countrymen, he and they would have
been flaves to this hour, and the Baftile had
ftill hung over the ill-fated city of Paris.
Is liberty a difeafe for which we are to be
prepared as for inoculation ; if fo, and if
fafting and abftinence, and long fuffering,
be preparation, there are no men under
Heaven better prepared than the Catholics
of Ireland.

But can we believe that our wife and
benevolent Creator would conftitute us fo,
that it would require a long inftitution to
prepare us for that bleffing, without which
exiftence is but a burthen ?

E   Do

Do we prepare our fons to view the light of Heaven, to breathe the air, to tread the earth ?

LIBERTY is the vital principle of man: He that is prepared to live, is prepared for freedom.

WHATEVER is effential to the happy exiftence of his creatures, God has not willed fhould be difficult, or complex, or doubtful in its preparation : Plant then, with a righteous confidence in his goodnefs, the vigorous fhoot of liberty in the land, and doubt not, but it fhall ftrike root, and flourifh, and fpread, until the whole people fhall repofe beneath its fhade in peace and happinefs, and glory.

BUT it is objected, that certain tenets expreffive of unconftitutional fubmiffion to their Holy Father, the Pope, in temporal as well as fpiritual matters, is a fufficient ground for excluding the Roman Catholics from their rights. " If this were fo, it " were a grievous fault," and I may add, " grievoufly has .Ireland anfwered it." But whatever truth there might have been in fuch an accufation in the dark ages of fuperftition, when, by the bye, Ireland did but fhare the blame with England, and all Europe ;

Europe; yet now, in the days of illumination, at the clofe of the eighteenth century, fuch an opinion is too monftrous to obtain a moment's ferious belief, unlefs with fuch as were determined to believe every thing which fquared with their interefted views : The beft anfwer to fuch a calumny, if indeed it deferves any, is the conduct of the Catholics of England at this day, and their folemn declaration figned by their Gentry, their Clergy, and their Peers, fanctified befides by the unanimous decifions of feven of the firft Catholic Univerfities in Europe, including that of Salamanca, of Valladolid, of Doway, and the Sorbonne * ; wherein they concur in afferting, that neither the Pope and Cardinals, nor even a general Council, have the fmalleft pretenfion to interfere between Prince and Subject, as to allegiance or temporal matters. And I hope, as thefe opinions are folemnly given from Catholics to Catholics, they may have the fortune to efcape the old and wicked cenfure, that, " *faith is not to be kept with heretics.*"

---

* See Lord Petre's letter to the Bifhop of St. David's.

IT

IT is not fix months fince the Pope was publicly burned in effigy at Paris, the capital of that Monarch, whois ftiled the eldeft fon of the church. Yet the time has been, when Philip of France thought he had a good title to the Crown of England, from the donation of the Holy Father: The fallacy lies in fuppcling that what was once true in politics, is always true : I do believe the Pope has now more power in Ireland than in fome Catholic countries, or than he perhaps ought to have. But I confefs, I look on his power with little apprehenfion, becaufe I cannot fee to what evil purpofe it could be exerted; and with the lefs apprehenfion, as every liberal extenfion of property or franchife to Catholics will tend to diminifh it. Perfecution will keep alive the foolifh bigotry and fuperftiticn of any fect, as the experience of five thoufand years has demonftrated. Perfecution bound the Irifh Papift to his Prieft, and the Prieft to the Pope ; the bond of union is drawn tighter by oppreffion ; relaxation will undo it. The emancipated and liberal Irifhman, like the emancipated and liberal Frenchman, may go to mafs, may tell his beads, or fprinkle

his

his miftrefs with holy water; but neither the one nor the other will attend to the rufty and extinguifhed thunderbolts of the Vatican, or the idle anathemas, which indeed his Holinefs is now-a-days too prudent and cautious to iffue.

I COME now to an old and hackneyed argument againft Irifh Catholics, that they are Jacobites, and for bringing in the Pretender: To this I have an hundred anfwers, but with fair reafoners, it is probable that the firft may be fufficient. I fay the man is dead; there is no Pretender: His brother, who furvives him, is in religion, a Cardinal, a Popifh Clergyman; and what is fome additional ground to think, he may not have lawful, or indeed any iffue, is, that he is above fixty years of age: If however, any ftrenuous Proteftant is diffatisfied with this anfwer as inconclufive, let him ftate his objections, and I fhall, perhaps, in the tenth edition of my book, fet myfelf to remove them. In the mean time, let him confider, that fince the acceffion of the Houfe of Brunfwick, there have been two bloody rebellions on behalf of the Stuart family in England; but not one fword or trigger drawn in the caufe in Ireland.

ANOTHER

ANOTHER argument that has been often fuccefsfully ufed, is this: If the Catholics are admitted to franchife, they will get the upper hand, and attach themfelves to France, *for Ireland is unable to exift as an independent State !* But France is a Popifh country, and ruled by an abfolute Monarch, whofe will is the law; therefore it is better to remain in a ftate of qualified freedom, though it be not complete, under the protection of England, than fink into a province to France; *for to one or the other you muft be content to be fubject.*

THERE is no one pofition, moral, phyfical, or political, that I hear with fuch extreme exacerbation of mind, as this which denies to my country the poffibility of independent exiftence : It is not however, my plan here to examine that queftion : I truft, whenever the neceffity does arife, as at fome time it infallibly muft, it will be found that we are as competent to our own government, regulation *and defence,* as any State in Europe. Till the emergency does occur, it will but exafperate and inflame the minds of men, to inveftigate and demonftrate the infinite refources and provocations to independence, which every hour brings

brings forth in Ireland. I shall therefore
here content myself with protesting on behalf of my country, against the position,
as an infamous falsehood, insulting to her
pride, and derogatory to her honour ; and
I little doubt, if occasion should arise, but
that I shall be able to prove it so.

To the argument founded on this spirit-
less and pitiful position, time has given
an answer, by bringing forth that stupen-
dous event, the Revolution in France, an
event which I do but name, for who is he
that can praise it as it merits ? Where is
the dread now of absolute power, or the
arbitrary nod of the Monarch in France ?
Where is the intolerance of Popish bigotry ? The rights of man are at least as well
understood there as here, and somewhat
better practised. Their wife and venera-
ble National Assembly, representatives, not
of their constituents, merely but of man,
whose nature they have exalted beyond the
limits that even Providence seemed to have
bounded it by, have with that disinterest-
ed attention to the true welfare of their
species, which has marked and dignified
all their proceedings, renounced the idea
of conquest, and engraven that renunciation

on

on the altar, in the temple of their liberty : In that Affembly Proteftants fit indifcriminately with Catholics : But I lofe time in dwelling on circumftances, the mention of which at once fuperfedes the neceffity of argument.

I COME now to a very ferious argument. If you admit Catholics to vote, you muft admit them to the Houfe, and then you will have a Catholic Parliament. To this there are many anfwers : In the firft place, it is incumbent on their opponents to fhew the mifchief refulting from even a Catholic Parliament. There has been fo bold a fpirit, fo guarded a wifdom, fo pure a patriotifm exerted by a Parliament of Catholics in this kingdom, as the experience of modern Proteftant Parliaments can give us no conception of : Have we ever read, or have we forgotten the manifefto of the Catholic Parliament held at Trim, in 1642 ? Let it be compared with our own declarations in 1782, and Catholics may well, with a generous confidence, ftand the comparifon.

BUT it will be faid, that the laft Catholic Parliament which we faw, fet itfelf from the poft, to refume the forfeited lands, and

and repeal the act of fettlement. That Parliament was fummoned by King James II. at a time when his Proteftant fubjects had expelled him from his throne and king-dom. The Irifh Catholics with a gene-rous, though mifplaced loyalty, and with that ardent zeal which has on a thoufand occafions outrun their judgment, regarded their Proteftant Brethren, not merely as fectaries and fchifmatics, but as rebels to their lawful Prince, whom it was their duty as well as, perhaps, their inclination, to punifh by rigid confifcation: The for-feitures and transfer of property were then recent, moft of them within forty years. Many of the individuals who had been actually difpoffeffed, muft have been liv-ing; the fons of many more ; befides, it was a fudden and unhoped-for reftoration of power to men, whom it had been the policy of Proteftant afcendency for 150 years to deprefs ; and this reftoration ac-complifhed, not merely without the affift-ance, but abfolutely againft the confent of the Proteftants of Ireland. Is it to be won-dered at, under fuch circumftances, if the firft exertions of that power were guided rather by refentment and paffion, than rea-

F   fon?

fon ? Is Catholicity to blame, or human
nature ? But fee how different everything
is at this day ! Moft of the ancient Irifh
families are extinct : In the minds of the
few remaining, one hundred and ten years
of, peace have cooled all refentment;
to the poffeffions of their anceftors, the
law has barred their title, and it was law
before the Revolution : Their civil rights
will be not extorted, but reftored ; not
wrung by fortuitous violence, but impart-
ed with benevolent juftice. Their reftoration to the rank of man, will be a work of
peaceful contract, not of implacable war
with their Proteftant Brethren.

BUT if all barriers between the two religions were beaten down, fo far as civil
matters are concerned, if the odious dif-
tinction of Proteftant and Prefbyterian,
and Catholic, were abolifhed, and the
three great fects blended together, under
the common and facred title of Irifhman,
what intereft could a Catholic member of
Parliament have, diftinct from his Proteftant brother fitting on the fame bench, ex-
ercifing the fame function, bound by the
fame ties. Would liberty be lefs dear to
him, juftice lefs facred, property lefs va-
luable

luable, infamy lefs dreadful? If the Houfe of Commons were to be even wholly Catholic, ftill the other eftates of the realm, the Peers and the King would fufficiently preferve the balance. I have fuppofed in this argument, what I peremptorily refufe to admit, that the whole Houfe of Commons muft be Catholic, and that they would of neceffity follow fuch meafures as would be prejudicial to the Proteftant intereft. But the fact is, that when we confider the great difproportion of property, or in other words power, in favour of the Proteftants, added to the weight and influence of Government, there can be little fear of a majority of Catholic members exifting in Parliament; and we know by hiftorical experience, that when the Houfe was open to both religions indifferently, no fuch majority exifted, though in times when Catholicity flourifhed, and the Proteftant intereft was feeble, comparatively, to what we fee at this day.

. IF however, there be ferious grounds for dreading a majority of Catholics, they may be removed by a very obvious mode; extend the elective franchife to fuch Catholics only as have a freehold of 10l. by

the

the year; and on the other hand, ſtrike off that diſgrace to our Conſtitution and our country, the wretched tribe of forty ſhilling freeholders, whom we ſee driven to their octennial market, by their land-lords, as much their property as the ſheep or the bullocks which they brand with their names. Thus will you at one ſtroke purge yourſelves of the groſs and feculent maſs which contaminates the Proteſtant in-tereſt, and reſtore their natural and juſt weight to the ſound and reſpectable part of the Catholic community, without throwing into their hands ſo much power as might enable them to dictate the law; but I again and again proteſt, that I conceive there is not a ſhadow of ground for ſuch ap-prehenſion; but other men may be more cautious than I, and I would wiſh to ob-viate and ſatisfy the apprehenſions of the moſt timid.

For my own part, I ſee Proteſtantiſm is no guard againſt corruption; I ſee the moſt profligate venality, the moſt ſhame-leſs and avowed proſtitution of principle go forward year after year, in aſſemblies, where no Catholic can by law appear: I ſee the people plundered and deſpiſed,

powerleſs

powerlefs and ridiculous, held in contempt and defiance, and with fuch a profpect before my eyes, I for one, feel little dread at the thoughts of change, where no change can eafily be for the worfe. Religion has at this day little influence on politics ; and when I contraft the National Affembly of Frenchmen and Catholics, with other great Bodies which I could name, I confefs, I feel little propenfity to boaft that I have the honour to be an Irifhman, and a Proteftant.

I HAVE now examined fuch arguments as are moft generally ufed to glofs over that monftrous injuftice which has held for a century three millions of my countrymen in ignorance and bondage. I have endeavoured to give them fuch anfwers, as a very plain underftanding could furnifh ; and I have a confidence that my attempt is but a precurfor of many efforts, more worthy of the merits of the caufe. The dark cloud which has fo long enveloped the Irifh Catholic with hopelefs mifery, at length begins to break, and the fun of liberty may once more illuminate his mind, and elevate his heart.

I HAVE

I HAVE hitherto confidered the cafe of the Catholics in the view of expediency, and as with reference to Proteftants I have done fo, becaufe I confefs I was afraid of the lengths to which reafon would inevitably lead me, if I were to take it up as a queftion of mere right, and with reference to the feelings of the Catholics themfelves : They have remained now for above a century in flavery; they may have loft the wifh for freedom ; and at any rate, I am not very fure that the man is their friend, who points out to them their mifery, and their degradation, at a time when it is not phyfically certain that their complete emancipation fhall immediately follow : Perhaps even this feeble attempt on their behalf, may prejudice the caufe which it is meant to defend. If it fhould be fo, I may lament; but I fhall never wifh to recall it.

WHAT anfwer could we make to the Catholics of Ireland, if they were to rife, and with one voice, demand their rights as Citizens, and as Men ? What reply juftifiable to God, and to our confcience? None. We prate and babble, and write books, and publifh them, filled with fentiments of freedom,

freedom, and abhorrence of tyranny, and lofty praifes of *the Rights of Man!* Yet we are content to hold three millions of our fellow creatures, and fellow fubjects, in degradation and infamy, and contempt, or to fum up all in one word, in *Slavery!*

On what chapter of the *Rights of Man*, do we ground our title to liberty, in the moment that we are riveting the fetters of the wretched Roman Catholics of Ireland. Shall they not fay to us, " Are we not men, as ye are, ftamped with the image of our Maker, walking erect, beholding the fame light, breathing the fame air as Proteftants : Hath not a Catholic hands ; hath not a Catholic eyes, dimenfions, organs, paffions? Fed with the fame food, hurt by the fame weapons, healed by the fame means, warmed and cooled by the fame fummer and winter, as a Proteftant is. If ye prick us, do we not bleed ? If ye tickle us, do we not laugh ? If ye poifon us, do we not die ? And if ye injure us, *fhall we not revenge?* Hath a Catholic the mark of the beaft in his forehead, that he fhould wander over his native foil like the accurfed Cain, with his hand againft every man, and every man's hand againft him ?

God

God Almighty in his juft anger, vifits the fins of the fathers upon the children, not beyond the third or fourth generation, even of thofe that hate him ; and will nothing fhort of our eternal flavery fatisfy the un-mitigable rage of Proteftant oppreffion ? How have *we* offended ? The offence of our anceftors, was their property and their power ; we have neither ; they are long fince facrificed, and you are in undifputed poffeffion of the fpoil. Do not then grudge us exiftence, or that for which alone man fhould exift—Liberty : Say not that we are unprepared ; Liberty prepares her-felf : Say not that we are ignorant, left ye judge yourfelves. Why are we fo ? Enough has been done and fuffered by us to fatisfy not only juftice and law, but coward-ice, malice, and revenge ; it is time our perfecution fhould ceafe. The nations of Europe are vindicating themfelves into freedom ; ye talk about it yourfelves, and do ye think that we will be left behind : If you will join us, we are ready to embrace you ; if you will not, fhame and difcomfi-ture await you. For us, whether fupport-ed or not, we are prepared for either event. If Freedom comes, we will clafp her to

our

our hearts, and furrender her, but with
our laft breath ; if flavery is ftill to be our
portion, we have learned by bitter experience to endure ; and to that righteous and
juft God, who has created and preferves
us, we commit our caufe, nothing doubt-
ing, but in the fullnefs of his good time,
that he will manifeft his glorious mercies,
even unto us ; though for wife purpofes,
he may think fit to continue us a little
longer under the rod of our oppreffors, the
minifters of his wrath."

IF fuch an appeal were made, *what
fhould we anfwer ?* Let him that can, devife a reply; I know of none.

THE argument now ftands thus : To
oppofe the unconftitutional weight of Government, fubject as that Government is
to the ftill more unconftitutional and unjuft bias of Englifh influence, it is abfolutely neceffary that the weight of the people's fcale fhould be encreafed. This object can only be attained by a Reform in
Parliament, and no reform is practicable,
that fhall not include the Catholics. Thefe
three fteps are infeparably connected, and
let not any man deceive himfelf, by fuppofing the firft attainable without the fecond, or either without the third. Is the

G   prefent

present Government of Ireland such an one as ought to be opposed? Every good Irishman will answer, yes! Have we not sufficient experience, how fruitless all opposition is on the present system? The people are divided, each party afraid and jealous of the other; they have only the justice of their cause to support them, and that plea grievously weakened by the acknowledged exclusion of three-fourths of the nation from their rights as men: Government, *a foreign Government*, is a small, but a disciplined and compact body, with the sword, the purse, and the honours of Ireland at their disposal: It is easy to see the event of such an opposition to such an Administration. It follows, that to oppose it with success, the people must change their plan.

Do we not see the conduct of Government at this hour, and shall we not learn wisdom, even from our enemies? They know that the Catholics hold the balance between them and that fraction of the nation, which we chuse to dignify with the name of *the People*; and therefore, they court the Catholics. If they secure them, I should be glad to know, what they have to fear with the immense power and influence attached to office, with the command

mand of the treafury, and with the whole
Catholic party, three-fourths of the kingdom, attached by gratitude to them, and
alienated by repeated fufpicion, and unre-
mitting ill ufage from their enemies.

In a word, the alternative is, on the one
hand Reform, and the Catholics, juftice and
liberty ; on the other, an unconditional
fubmiffion to the prefent, and every future
Adminiftration, who may think proper to
follow their fteps, and who may indulge
with eafe and fafety their propenfity to peculation and fpoil, and infult, while the
people remain timid and divided. Between thefe you muft chufe, and chufe immediately, and that choice may be final.

If the whole body of the people unite
with cordial fincerity, and demand a general Reform in Parliament, which fhall
include reftitution of the elective franchife
to the Catholics ; we fhall then, and not
otherwife, have an honeft and independent reprefentation of the people; we fhall
have a barrier of ftrength fufficient to defy
the utmoft efforts of the moft profligate
and powerful Englifh Adminiftration; we
fhall be enabled to avail ourfelves of the
infinite advantages with which Providence
has endowed our country; corruption fhall

be

beannihilated, Government fhall becomeho-
neft per-force, and thereby recover at leaft
fome of that refpectability which a long
courfe of political depravity has exhaufted :
In a word, we fhall recover our rank, and become a nation in fomething befide the name.

IF on the other hand, we think reform
too dear, when purchafed by juftice; if
we are ftill illiberal and blind bigots, who
deny that civil liberty can exift out of the
pale of Proteftantifm, if we with-hold the
facred cup of *Liberty* from our Catholic
Brother, and repel him from the
communion of our natural rights, let
us at leaft be confiftent, and ceafe to mur-
mur at the oppreffion of the Government
which grinds us; let us bear, if we can,
without wincing the whips and goads of
our own tyrants, with the confoling reflec-
tion, that we can act the tyrant in our turn,
and gall the wretched flaves below us; let
Adminiftration proceed to play upon the
terrors of the Proteftants, the hopes of the
Catholics, and balancing the one party
by the other, plunder and laugh at, and
defy both; let Englifh influence meet and
check our rifing commerce at every turn;
let us remain obfcure and wretched, and
unknown in Europe; let the bulk of the
people

people continue barbarians, in hopelefs and incurable ignorance, and wretchednefs, and want : All is well, fo long as we can prevent the Catholics from rifing to a rank in fociety with ourfelves ; we will, in the fpirit of the envious man in the fable, bear to lofe one of our eyes, fo that our neighbour may lofe both, and grope about in utter darknefs.

BUT I will hope better things : The example of America, of Poland, and above all, of France, cannot on the minds of liberal men but force conviction. In France 200,000 Catholics deputed a Proteftant, St. Etienne, to the National Affembly, as their reprefentative, with orders to procure, what has fince been accomplifhed, an abolition of all civil diftinctions, which were founded merely on religious opinions. In America, the Catholic and Proteftant fit equally in Congrefs, without any contention arifing, other than who fhall ferve his country beft : So may it be in Ireland ! So will it be, if men are fincere in their wifhes for her profperity and future elevation : Let them but confider what union has done in fmall ftates, what difcord in great ones : Let them look to their Government ; let them

look

look to their fellow flaves, who by coaliti-
on with them, may rife to be their fellow
citizens, and form a new order in their
fociety, a new era in their hiftory : Let
them once cry *Reform, and the Catholics* and
Ireland is free, independent, and happy.

A NORTHERN WHIG.

BELFAST, AUGUST 1, 1791.